Cybersecurity Made Simple

A Beginner's Guide to Protecting Your Digital Life

Curious Mind Press

FOREWORD

Welcome to "Cybersecurity Made Simple: A Beginner's Guide to Protecting Your Digital Life." We're excited to share this book with you because it's all about keeping your online world safe, and we promise, it's not as complicated as it might sound.

In today's world, we do so much online; shopping, chatting, learning, and more. But with all the good comes some challenges. There are people out there who want to trick us or mess with our digital lives. That's where cybersecurity comes in.

This book is your trusty guide through the digital jungle. It will show you how to make strong passwords that are like armor for your accounts. You'll learn how to spot tricky emails and websites that want to steal your information. Plus, we'll share some stories about real people who faced digital troubles.

But don't worry, this book isn't just about talking. It's about doing too. You'll find step-by-step instructions to keep your devices safe and your home network guarded. And we'll talk about things like privacy and social media, so you're in control of what you share.

Towards the end, we'll peek into the future to see what new challenges might come our way. But remember, you're not alone on this journey. By the time you finish reading, you'll be equipped with the knowledge and tools to stand strong in the digital world.

Let's dive in and discover how you can own your digital space and surf the web with confidence. Enjoy the book and remember: Stay curious, stay safe!

Warm regards,

Curious Mind Press

CONTENTS

CHAPTER 1: INTRODUCTION TO CYBERSECURITY

Meet Mary, a tech-savvy young professional who's always been careful online. One sunny morning, she gets an email that looks like it's from her bank. The message says there's been a 'security breach' and she needs to act fast.

Feeling a rush of worry, Mary clicks the link and fills in her account details, thinking she's doing the right thing. But here's the twist: that email was a sneaky trick!

Cybercriminals had sent it to steal her info. Suddenly, Mary's bank account isn't just hers anymore. She's facing strange transactions, her identity is in jeopardy, and she can't shake off the feeling of being tricked.

It's a digital rollercoaster she never saw coming.

In a world where digital technologies seamlessly intertwine with our daily lives, cybersecurity has emerged as a critical concern. From online banking to social media interactions, the digital landscape has expanded our horizons, but it has also introduced new vulnerabilities. This chapter marks the beginning of your journey into the realm of cybersecurity – a journey that will empower you to protect your digital life with confidence.

Setting the Stage

Picture this: you wake up to the sound of your smartphone's alarm. As you scroll through your social media feed, you stumble upon a news article discussing a major data breach that compromised the personal information of thousands of individuals. A chill runs down your spine as you realize that you, too, are part of this interconnected web of data.

Welcome to the interconnected era, where our devices, from phones to laptops to smart home appliances, are interwoven with the fabric of our lives. This connectivity has brought unprecedented convenience, but it also introduces new challenges, the foremost being the security of our digital presence. Our personal information – from emails and photos to financial records – is scattered across the digital realm, waiting to be safeguarded against potential threats.

Why This Book

As you read these words, you might be wondering, "Is cybersecurity really something I need to worry about?" The short answer is yes. Cybersecurity is no longer solely the concern of IT professionals and tech-savvy individuals. It's a concern that spans generations, backgrounds, and professions. Whether you're a student, a parent, a professional, or a retiree, your digital life is worth protecting.

But fear not – this book is here to make cybersecurity accessible and actionable for everyone. We understand that the world of cybersecurity can appear complex and intimidating, filled with jargon and technicalities. Our goal is to break down these barriers and provide you with a solid foundation to navigate the digital landscape with confidence.

Embrace Your Digital Journey

Your journey into the realm of cybersecurity starts here. By the time you reach the final pages of this book, you'll be empowered to take control of your digital life. You'll learn about the fundamental concepts that underpin cybersecurity, gain insights into the most prevalent threats, and acquire practical skills to fortify your online presence.

Remember, cybersecurity is not a destination; it's a continuous journey. With the knowledge and practices you'll acquire, you'll be better prepared to adapt to the ever-evolving digital landscape. The world of cybersecurity may be complex, but with the right guidance, it becomes manageable, approachable, and even empowering.

So, let's embark on this journey together. By understanding cybersecurity's core principles, you'll be well-equipped to protect your digital life, make informed decisions, and confidently navigate the vast expanse of the digital world. The next chapter will dive into the basics of cybersecurity, helping you build a strong foundation for the chapters to come. Get ready to unlock the doors to a safer digital existence.

CHAPTER 2: UNDERSTANDING THE BASICS

Meet Sarah, a dedicated professional and loving mom, who starts her day with an email that seems to be from her favorite online store. The message claims she's won an unbelievable prize and just needs to download an exciting attachment to claim it.

Thrilled, Sarah clicks without hesitation. But this seemingly innocent action sets off a chain of events she couldn't foresee. Unbeknownst to her, the attachment contained hidden ransomware, which swiftly locks up her files and demands a ransom for their release.

Panic sets in as Sarah realizes her precious family photos and work documents are held hostage by faceless cybercriminals.

Caught in a web of deceit, Sarah learns the hard way about the dangers lurking in the digital world. Her journey to regain control over her data and protect her family's online presence becomes a lesson in resilience and vigilance.

In the interconnected digital landscape of today, understanding the basics of cybersecurity is a fundamental step towards safeguarding your digital life. This chapter will delve into the core concepts of cybersecurity, shedding light on common cyber threats that individuals encounter and the importance of staying vigilant.

What is Cybersecurity?

In its essence, cybersecurity encompasses the measures taken to protect electronic systems, networks, and data from unauthorized access, attacks, and damage. It's not just a concern for governments and corporations; it directly impacts each one of us as we navigate the online realm.

Imagine your digital presence as a virtual extension of your physical life—a realm where sensitive information, personal communication, and valuable assets reside. Cybersecurity is the armor that shields you from the lurking dangers of the digital world, such as cybercriminals seeking to exploit vulnerabilities for financial gain or disrupt operations.

Common Cyber Threats

To understand the importance of cybersecurity, it's crucial to familiarize yourself with the common threats that can compromise your digital well-being:

o **Phishing Attacks:** Phishing is like the digital version of a con artist trying to trick you into revealing personal information, such as passwords, credit card details, or Social Security numbers. These attacks often come in the form of seemingly legitimate emails, messages, or websites that prompt you to take action.

o **Malware:** Short for malicious software, malware includes viruses, worms, Trojans, and spyware. These malicious programs can infect your devices and steal sensitive data or control your system without your knowledge.

o **Ransomware:** Ransomware encrypts your files and demands a ransom for their release. Falling victim to a ransomware attack can be devastating, as it can result in loss of important files and significant financial implications.

o **Data Breaches:** Data breaches occur when unauthorized individuals gain access to sensitive information stored by organizations. This can lead to identity theft, financial loss, and privacy violations.

o **Social Engineering:** Social engineering involves manipulating individuals into divulging confidential information. It can take the form of a phone call, email, or in-person interaction, with the goal of exploiting human psychology to gain access to information.

In the upcoming chapters, we will delve deeper into strategies to shield yourself from these threats and empower you to take control of your digital life. Remember, knowledge is your strongest weapon in the battle against cyber threats. By building a strong foundation of cybersecurity awareness, you are taking the first step towards securing your online presence.

CHAPTER 3: STRONG AND SECURE PASSWORDS

Introducing Fatima, a dedicated student with a passion for showcasing her creativity on her online portfolio. Eager to share her artistry with the world, she poured hours into building her digital haven. Little did she know that a storm was brewing in the digital shadows.

One day, as Fatima excitedly checked her email, she was hit by a shockwave of realization. Her account had been infiltrated, a virtual break-in that left her feeling violated. How did this happen? It turned out her password was as fragile as a house of cards. With a swift hack, her email fortress crumbled.

The consequences were swift and distressing. Unwelcome visitors sneaked into her social media realm, wreaking havoc by posting unauthorized content. Her online projects, once a source of pride, fell victim to digital vandals. Worst of all, her private documents were no longer private, scattered like leaves in the wind.

In the vast realm of the digital landscape, passwords serve as the guardians of our online identity and personal information. They are the virtual keys that lock and unlock the doors to our digital lives. Whether it's accessing your email, managing your bank accounts, or connecting with friends on social media, passwords play a pivotal role in ensuring the security of your online interactions. In this chapter, we delve into the world of strong and secure passwords, exploring why they are essential, how to create them, and the tools that can make managing them a breeze.

Importance of Passwords

Imagine walking down a crowded street, leaving your front door wide open for anyone to enter. Unthinkable, right? However, in the digital world, many of us inadvertently leave our virtual doors unlocked by using weak and easily guessable passwords. This is an open invitation for cybercriminals to gain unauthorized access to our sensitive information, leading to identity theft, financial loss, and other online havoc.

A strong password acts as a robust lock that resists even the most persistent of virtual intruders. It forms the first line of defense against unauthorized access to your accounts, whether it's your email, social media, or online banking. A secure password is a combination of letters, numbers, symbols, and case variations that are seemingly random and challenging to guess. By using strong passwords, you substantially decrease the risk of falling victim to cyberattacks.

Creating Strong Passwords

Creating a strong password might seem like a daunting task, but it's far simpler than you might think. One approach is to create a passphrase—an easy-to-remember sequence of words or phrases that hold personal significance to you. These words are combined with numbers and symbols to enhance their complexity.

For instance, consider a phrase like "I love hiking in the mountains." To transform this into a strong password, you could use the first letter of each word along with some variations: "ILh1km#2023". This passphrase-derived password is not only strong but also memorable, making it easier for you to recall without resorting to jotting it down.

Password Managers: Your Digital Gatekeepers

Remembering numerous complex passwords for the ever-growing list of online accounts can quickly become overwhelming. This is where password managers step in as your digital gatekeepers. A password manager is a software tool that securely stores your passwords, automatically generates strong ones, and fills them in for you when needed.

Leading password managers, such as LastPass, Dashlane, and 1Password, offer a range of features that simplify the password management process. They generate complex passwords for you, store them in an encrypted vault, and automatically fill them in when you visit a website or app. This not only streamlines your online experience but also eliminates the need to use the same password across multiple accounts—a practice that significantly increases your vulnerability.

Setting Up a Password Manager
Let's walk through the process of setting up a password manager using LastPass as an example:

o **Choose a Password Manager:** Visit the LastPass website and sign up for an account. You'll need to create a master password, which is the one password you'll need to remember—make sure it's strong and unique.

o **Install the Browser Extension:** Download and install the LastPass browser extension. This extension integrates seamlessly with your web browser, making it easy to manage and autofill passwords as you browse the internet.

o **Save and Generate Passwords:** As you log in to different websites, LastPass will offer to save your passwords. Whenever you need to create a new password, LastPass can generate a strong one for you and store it in your vault.

o **Access Your Vault:** To access your saved passwords, log in to your LastPass account through the browser extension or the mobile app. You can organize passwords into folders, update them, and even share them securely with trusted contacts.

Mastering the Art of Password Security
While using a password manager is a significant step toward bolstering your online security, there are a few additional practices to keep in mind:

o **Unique Passwords:** Each online account should have a unique password. This way, if one account is compromised, your other accounts remain secure.

o **Two-Factor Authentication (2FA):** Enable 2FA for your accounts whenever possible. This adds an extra layer of security by requiring a secondary form of verification, such as a code sent to your phone, in addition to your password.

o **Regular Updates:** Periodically update your passwords, especially for critical accounts like email and banking. This minimizes the risk of an attacker gaining prolonged access.

Conclusion
In the digital age, the concept of a "key" has transformed into the realm of passwords—a key that holds the power to protect or expose our virtual existence. The importance of strong and secure passwords cannot be overstated. They are the foundation of your online security, guarding your personal data and digital assets from malicious actors. By creating strong passwords, utilizing password managers, and embracing other password security practices, you're not just enhancing your digital life—you're actively participating in the collective effort to fortify the digital world against cyber threats.

CHAPTER 4: RECOGNIZING PHISHING AND SOCIAL ENGINEERING

Meet Alex, a tech-savvy freelance graphic designer who's always on the lookout for new opportunities. One day, as he was scrolling through his emails, he noticed a message that seemed too good to be true. The subject line read, "Exclusive Design Project: High-Paying Gig Inside!" Intrigued, Alex eagerly opened the email.

The message claimed to be from a prestigious design agency and offered him a dream project with a jaw-dropping payout. Excitement bubbled up within him, and without a second thought, he clicked the link provided to "learn more." The link took him to a login page that perfectly mimicked the agency's website.

Eager to seize this golden opportunity, Alex entered his login credentials. As the page loaded, he realized he might have made a mistake. An uneasy feeling settled in as he saw the URL was slightly off. Suddenly, it dawned on him that he might have fallen for a phishing trap.

In the vast landscape of cyber threats, phishing stands out as one of the most prevalent and effective tactics used by cybercriminals to compromise your security. Unlike many other cyber attacks that rely on sophisticated coding or advanced hacking techniques, phishing leverages human psychology to manipulate individuals into divulging sensitive information, such as passwords, credit card numbers, or personal details. This chapter will delve into the world of phishing, exploring its tactics, red flags, and strategies to protect yourself from falling victim.

Understanding Phishing

Phishing is a digital form of social engineering that aims to trick individuals into revealing confidential information by masquerading as a legitimate source. Cybercriminals often impersonate trusted entities like banks, email providers, or even government agencies to gain victims' trust. The term "phishing" is derived from the analogy of casting a wide net, hoping to catch unsuspecting individuals like fish.

Anatomy of a Phishing Attack

Phishing attacks can take various forms, but they typically involve the following stages:

o **Baiting:** The attacker lures victims using enticing offers, discounts, or false promises. This could be in the form of an email, SMS, social media message, or even a fake website.

o **Hooking:** Once the victim engages, the attacker employs psychological tactics to create a sense of urgency, fear, or curiosity. This is where emotions come into play, clouding judgment and leading to hasty actions.

o **Reeling In:** The victim is directed to a fraudulent website that closely resembles a legitimate one. Here, they're prompted to provide sensitive information such as usernames, passwords, credit card numbers, or personal details.

o **Exfiltration:** Armed with the stolen data, the attacker can carry out various malicious activities, from stealing money to conducting identity theft.

Spotting Red Flags

Phishing attacks are often sophisticated and designed to deceive, but there are telltale signs that can help you identify them:

o **Unusual Sender Addresses:** Legitimate organizations typically use official domain names for their email addresses. Be wary of addresses that use misspellings, subdomains, or variations of the real domain.

o **Urgent and Threatening Language:** Phishing emails often employ urgency and fear to compel immediate action. If an email claims your account will be closed, or you'll face legal consequences unless you act immediately, take a step back and evaluate the situation.

o **Suspicious Links:** Hover your mouse over any links in the email without clicking on them. Check if the link matches the displayed text or if it redirects to an unfamiliar URL. Be cautious of shortened URLs, as they can hide the true destination.

o **Poor Grammar and Spelling:** Many phishing emails contain spelling mistakes, grammatical errors, or awkward phrasing. These errors can indicate that the email was hastily put together and not from a reputable source.

o **Generic Greetings:** Phishing emails often use generic greetings like "Dear Customer" instead of addressing you by name. Legitimate organizations typically personalize their communications.

o **Requests for Sensitive Information:** Legitimate companies won't ask you to provide sensitive information like passwords, credit card numbers, or Social Security numbers via email. If an email asks for such information, treat it as suspicious.

o **Unexpected Attachments:** Attachments from unknown sources can contain malware. Don't open attachments unless you're expecting them and can verify the sender's authenticity.

Protecting Yourself from Phishing

To protect yourself from phishing you can take the following measures:

o **Stay Calm and Think Before You Click:** When you receive an email that demands immediate action, take a moment to assess the situation. Scammers rely on your emotional response to bypass your rational thinking.

o **Verify the Sender's Identity:** If you receive an email from your bank, for example, visit the official website directly by typing the URL into your browser. Don't rely on links provided in emails.

o **Check the URL:** Always hover over links before clicking them to see where they lead. If the link doesn't match the text or seems unusual, don't click on it.

o **Use Multi-Factor Authentication (MFA):** MFA adds an extra layer of security by requiring you to provide more than just a password to access your accounts. Even if a hacker obtains your password, they won't be able to access your account without the additional authentication factor.

o **Educate Yourself and Others:** Spread awareness about phishing among your friends, family, and colleagues. The more people understand the risks, the more difficult it becomes for scammers to succeed.

o **Use Security Software:** Install reputable security software that can detect and block phishing attempts. These tools often have built-in features that warn you about potentially malicious websites.

Conclusion

Phishing attacks thrive on exploiting human psychology, but armed with knowledge, you can recognize their tricks and protect yourself. Remember, cybercriminals may constantly change their tactics, but by staying vigilant and practicing cautious online behavior, you can significantly reduce your risk of falling victim to these devious schemes.

CHAPTER 5: SAFE BROWSING HABITS

Meet Aisha, an adventurous traveler with a passion for exploring new places. While planning her next getaway, she stumbled upon a travel forum that promised insider tips on off-the-beaten-path destinations. Eager to discover hidden gems, Aisha excitedly clicked on a link that claimed to reveal "Top 10 Undiscovered Islands You Must Visit."

As the webpage loaded, a flurry of pop-up ads appeared, urging her to download a suspicious-looking travel guide. Undeterred, Aisha was determined to find her dream travel spot and clicked on the download button. Almost instantly, her screen froze, and a message popped up, demanding payment to unlock her device.

Panicked and frustrated, Aisha realized she had fallen into a trap. She had unknowingly stumbled upon a website ridden with malware, cunningly disguised as a treasure trove of travel insights. Her eagerness to explore new destinations had led her straight into the hands of cybercriminals.

In the digital age, browsing the internet has become an integral part of our lives. From social media and online shopping to research and entertainment, the web offers a wealth of information and experiences. However, this convenience comes with its own set of risks. Malicious websites, phishing attacks, and online trackers are just a few of the threats that can compromise your online security and privacy. In this chapter, we'll explore safe browsing habits and equip you with the tools you need to navigate the online landscape securely.

Secure Websites: The Foundation of Safe Browsing

The first step to safe browsing is recognizing and using secure websites. A secure website is indicated by the "https://" prefix in the URL and a padlock icon in the browser's address bar. The "s" in "https" stands for "secure," indicating that the connection between your device and the website is encrypted. This encryption helps prevent hackers from intercepting your data and sensitive information.

When you visit a website that requires you to input personal or financial information, such as when making an online purchase or logging into your email account, always ensure that the website is secure. Avoid entering sensitive data on websites without the "https://" prefix, as these sites lack the encryption necessary to protect your information.

Avoiding Suspicious Links: Think Before You Click

One of the most common ways cybercriminals target unsuspecting users is through malicious links. These links can lead to phishing websites, malware downloads, or other forms of cyberattacks. To avoid falling victim to these threats, adopt a "think before you click" mindset:

o **Hover Over Links:** Before clicking on a link, hover your mouse cursor over it to preview the URL. This allows you to see the actual destination of the link. If the URL looks suspicious or doesn't match the website's official domain, refrain from clicking.

o **Be Cautious of Unsolicited Emails:** Phishing emails often contain links that claim to lead to legitimate websites. However, these emails are designed to deceive you. If you receive an email from an unfamiliar sender or with an unexpected attachment or link, exercise caution.

o **Type URLs Manually:** If you're unsure about the legitimacy of a link, it's safer to type the URL of the website directly into your browser's address bar. This eliminates the risk of clicking on a malicious link.

o **Verify Sources:** If a link is shared with you through social media, messaging apps, or other platforms, verify the source before clicking. Cybercriminals often use social engineering tactics to trick users into clicking on harmful links.

Ad-Blockers and Pop-up Blockers: Guarding Against Malicious Ads
Online advertisements are a common feature of many websites, but they can also be used to spread malware and redirect users to malicious websites. Ad-blockers and pop-up blockers are tools that can help you mitigate these risks:

o **Ad-Blockers:** Browser extensions and plugins like AdBlock and uBlock Origin can prevent ads from displaying on websites. These tools not only enhance your browsing experience by reducing clutter but also protect you from potentially harmful ads.

o **Pop-up Blockers:** Pop-up blockers prevent intrusive pop-up windows from opening automatically. Cybercriminals often use pop-ups to trick users into downloading malware or revealing sensitive information. By using a pop-up blocker, you reduce your exposure to these threats.

Conclusion: Navigating the Digital Seas Safely
Safe browsing habits are the foundation of a secure online experience. By recognizing secure websites, avoiding suspicious links, and using tools like ad-blockers and pop-up blockers, you can significantly reduce your risk of falling victim to cyber threats. Remember, every click matters, and taking a moment to evaluate the safety of a link or website can save you from potential harm. In the next chapter, we'll delve into another critical aspect of cybersecurity: securing your devices to protect your digital life.

CHAPTER 6: SECURING YOUR DEVICES

Introducing Jake, a tech enthusiast eager to try new things. One day, he stumbled upon a shiny free software while browsing the web. Intrigued, he swiftly downloaded it, expecting a digital adventure. Little did he realize, this software harbored a hidden enemy – malware, a digital spy.

At first, Jake's computer seemed okay, but soon it became a sloth, moving at a snail's pace. Baffled, he noticed mysterious pop-ups invading his screen like uninvited guests. Jake's excitement turned to concern as his computer woes escalated.

Unbeknownst to Jake, the malware was busy at work, sneaking into his digital secrets. Then, like a thief in the night, it stole his personal information – passwords, pictures, everything.

What Jake didn't know was that his prized possessions were auctioned off on the dark web, leaving him to grapple with the aftermath.

In today's interconnected world, our devices serve as gateways to our digital lives. From smartphones and laptops to tablets and smart TVs, these devices store valuable personal information and provide access to various online services. However, they are also susceptible to cyber threats. In this chapter, we'll explore how to secure your devices, keep them up to date, and use security software effectively.

The Importance of Device Security
Imagine waking up one morning to find that your laptop has been compromised, and your personal files are inaccessible. Unfortunately, this scenario isn't uncommon. Cybercriminals are constantly devising new ways to exploit vulnerabilities in devices and software. This is why it's crucial to take proactive steps to secure your devices.

Keeping Devices Up to Date
One of the simplest yet most effective ways to bolster device security is to keep everything up to date. Manufacturers regularly release software updates to address security vulnerabilities and improve overall functionality. Follow these steps to ensure your devices are up to date:

o **Operating System Updates:** Enable automatic updates for your operating system (e.g., Windows, macOS, Android, iOS). These updates often include security patches.

o **App Updates:** Regularly update apps on your devices. Cybercriminals can exploit vulnerabilities in outdated apps.

o **Firmware Updates:** For devices like routers and smart home devices, regularly check for firmware updates from the manufacturer.

Antivirus and Security Software
Antivirus and security software act as shields against a wide range of threats, from viruses to phishing attempts. Here's how to effectively use them:

o **Choose Reputable Software:** Opt for well-known and trusted security software providers. Research reviews and ratings before making a choice.

o **Install and Configure:** Install the software on your device and configure it according to your preferences. Some software offers real-time scanning, firewall protection, and more.

o **Scan Regularly:** Perform regular full-system scans. These scans help identify and remove any malicious files that might have slipped through.

Step-by-Step: Installing and Using Security Software
To illustrate, let's walk through the process of installing and using security software on a computer:

o **Research and Download:** Search for reputable security software providers and read reviews. Visit the provider's official website and download the software.

o **Install and Configure:** Run the installer and follow the on-screen instructions. Configure the software settings. Enable real-time scanning and automatic updates.

o **Scan:** Perform a full-system scan to identify existing threats. Set up regular custom scans for specific folders or files.

o **Safe Browsing:** Many security software options include browser extensions to warn about malicious websites.

By taking these steps, you're creating a strong defense against potential cyber threats.

Conclusion
Securing your devices is a fundamental step toward safeguarding your digital life. Regularly updating your devices and using reputable security software can greatly reduce your risk of falling victim to cyberattacks. Remember, just as you lock your front door to protect your home, you must lock your devices to protect your digital space. In the next chapter, we'll delve into another crucial aspect of cybersecurity: protecting your personal data.

CHAPTER 7: PROTECTING PERSONAL DATA

Meet Juan, an urban explorer and photography enthusiast. He loved capturing the hidden gems of his city and sharing them on social media. Every weekend, he embarked on a new adventure, checking in at trendy coffee shops, art galleries, and local landmarks.

Little did Juan know, his passion for sharing his whereabouts was gradually turning into a digital breadcrumb trail. A tech-savvy identity thief noticed Juan's routine and began connecting the dots. From his check-ins, the thief deduced Juan's favorite hangouts, his daily commute, and even his frequent travel destinations.

As weeks passed, Juan started receiving odd messages from unknown numbers. Strangers seemed to know personal details about his life, and he couldn't shake the feeling of being watched. Then, one day, he realized his bank account had been compromised, and unauthorized transactions were draining his funds.

In today's interconnected digital landscape, personal data has become a valuable commodity. From our online shopping habits to the photos we share on social media, every digital interaction leaves a trace. This chapter delves into the world of data privacy and offers guidance on how to protect your personal information in an increasingly data-driven world.

The Value of Personal Data
Imagine your personal data as pieces of a puzzle that, when assembled, create a comprehensive picture of your life. Advertisers, marketers, and even cybercriminals seek these puzzle pieces to target you more effectively. Your data is valuable, and maintaining control over it is crucial.

The Vulnerability of Personal Data
Consider the following scenarios:

o **Online Shopping:** When you make a purchase online, your transaction history and preferences can be collected and analyzed.

o **Social Media:** The posts you share, the people you interact with, and your interests are all valuable information.

o **Location Data:** Apps on your smartphone can track your movements, revealing your favorite places and routines.

o **Health Apps:** Fitness apps might track your exercise routines, sleep patterns, and even heart rate.

The concern is not about collecting data itself but rather who has access to it and how it's used. Companies may use your data to improve their services, tailor advertisements, or sell insights to third parties. On the darker side, cybercriminals might exploit your data for financial gain or even identity theft.

Safeguarding Your Digital Footprint
The following methods can help you to reduce your digital footprint:

o **Understand Privacy Policies:** Before using any online service or app, take a moment to read its privacy policy. This document outlines how your data will be collected, used, and shared. Understanding these policies empowers you to make informed decisions about the services you use and the data you share.

o **Limit Data Sharing:** Not all data needs to be shared. When signing up for a service, consider whether certain information is required. For example, does a social media site need your birthdate? Limiting the information you provide reduces your digital footprint.

o **Adjust Social Media Privacy Settings:** Social media platforms are virtual hubs of personal information, making them prime targets for data mining. Fortunately, most platforms offer privacy settings that allow you to control who sees your posts, photos, and personal details.

Step-by-Step Example: Adjusting Facebook Privacy Settings

o **Access Settings:** Click on the small arrow in the upper right corner of the Facebook page and select "Settings & Privacy."

o **Privacy Checkup:** Run the Privacy Checkup tool to review and adjust your privacy settings.

o **Who Can See Your Posts:** Choose who can see your future posts, either "Friends" or a customized group.

o **Timeline and Tagging:** Review who can post on your timeline and who can see posts you're tagged in.

o **Apps and Websites:** Remove any apps or websites that no longer need access to your Facebook data.

Location Services: The Benefits and Risks

Smartphones are equipped with GPS capabilities that allow apps to track your location. While this feature offers conveniences like navigation and local recommendations, it also raises privacy concerns.

The Benefits of Location Sharing include:

o **Navigation:** GPS-enabled apps guide you to your destination efficiently.

o **Local Recommendations:** Apps like Yelp suggest nearby restaurants and attractions.

o **Emergency Services:** Your location can be shared with emergency responders when needed.

The Risks of Location Sharing are:

o **Stalking and Harassment:** Sharing your location can make you vulnerable to unwanted attention.

o **Data Collection:** Apps might track your movements for advertising purposes.

o **Security Risks:** Sharing your location can expose your routines, making you a target for theft.

Step-by-Step: Managing Location Services on Your Smartphone

o **App Permissions:** Go to your smartphone's settings and find the app permissions section.

o **Location:** Review which apps have access to your location. Disable access for apps that don't require it.

o **Location History:** Some apps track your location history. Disable this feature if you're uncomfortable with it.

o **App-specific Settings:** Some apps allow you to choose when they can access your location, such as only when using the app.

Conclusion

Protecting your personal data is an ongoing process that requires vigilance and awareness. By understanding the value of your data, learning how to adjust privacy settings on social media platforms, and carefully considering the risks and benefits of location sharing, you can take control of your digital footprint. Remember, your data belongs to you, and safeguarding it is an essential step toward a more secure digital life.

In the next chapter, we'll explore safe social media usage, including strategies to avoid oversharing and steps to maintain a positive online presence.

CHAPTER 8: SAFE SOCIAL MEDIA USAGE

Meet Emily, an enthusiastic social media user who loved sharing snippets of her life online. From mouthwatering meals to scenic vacations, her posts painted a vibrant digital portrait. Little did she know, her seemingly harmless updates were attracting more than just likes.

One day, Emily received a friend request from a charming stranger named Alex. Flattered by the attention, she accepted without a second thought. They exchanged messages, and soon Alex knew about her favorite coffee shop, her pet's name, and even her upcoming vacation plans.

As Emily posted about her travels, Alex's interest grew, and he seemed to know a lot more than he should. Then came a shocking revelation: a picture from her vacation was edited to display her home address, posing a chilling question – how did Alex know?

In today's interconnected world, social media platforms have become an integral part of our lives. They allow us to connect with friends, share experiences, and express ourselves. However, the convenience of social media also comes with potential risks to our privacy and security. In this chapter, we'll explore the importance of safe social media usage and provide practical steps to protect your personal information.

The Pitfalls of Oversharing

Oversharing on social media can have serious consequences. Criminals and malicious actors can exploit the information you share to target you for scams, theft, or even physical harm. By revealing your current location and schedule, you make it easier for someone to track your movements. This is especially concerning when combined with the fact that your posts might be visible to a wide audience, including people you don't know personally.

Protecting Your Privacy

To enjoy the benefits of social media while safeguarding your personal information, you need to take proactive steps to manage your privacy settings. Here's how:

○ **Audit Your Friends and Followers:** Regularly review your friends or followers list. If you don't recognize someone, it's a good idea to remove them from your connections. Remember, your posts can potentially be seen by anyone in your network.

o **Control Your Audience:** Social media platforms often allow you to customize who sees your posts. Use this feature to share content only with people you trust. Consider creating different friend groups or lists for more granular control.

o **Review and Adjust Privacy Settings:**

- *Facebook:* On Facebook, click on the arrow in the top-right corner, then select "Settings & Privacy" > "Privacy Checkup." This tool guides you through your privacy settings, allowing you to adjust who can see your future posts, review tags before they appear on your timeline, and limit the audience for your past posts.

- *Instagram:* Go to your profile, tap the three lines in the top-right corner, then choose "Settings" > "Privacy." Here, you can set your account to private, control who can comment on your posts, and manage who can tag you.

- *Twitter:* Click on your profile picture, then choose "Settings and privacy" > "Privacy and safety." Here, you can set your tweets to be protected, limit who can tag you in photos, and control who can see your location.

- *LinkedIn:* Click on your profile picture, then select "Settings & Privacy" > "Privacy." Adjust your settings for who can see your connections, profile photo, and activity feed.

o **Be Mindful of Geotagging:** Many social media platforms allow you to add your location to posts. While this can be fun for sharing travel experiences, it also reveals your whereabouts. Consider disabling location tagging for sensitive posts or limiting it to a general area instead of specific coordinates.

o **Think Twice Before Accepting Friend Requests:** Just because you receive a friend request doesn't mean you have to accept it. Be cautious and only connect with people you know personally or have a legitimate reason to trust.

o **Beware of Third-Party Apps:** Some apps request access to your social media accounts. Before granting access, consider whether the app's purpose is legitimate and whether it truly needs your personal information.

o **Regularly Review App Permissions:** Apps you've connected to your social media accounts might have access to your personal data. Periodically review and revoke permissions for apps you no longer use or trust.

Conclusion

Safe social media usage is about finding a balance between enjoying the benefits of connectivity and protecting your personal information. By being mindful of what you share and taking control of your privacy settings, you can reduce the risks associated with oversharing. Remember that you have the power to shape your online presence and keep your digital life secure. Take the time to review and adjust your settings regularly, and encourage your friends and family to do the same. With a few simple steps, you can enjoy social media while safeguarding your privacy.

CHAPTER 9: SECURING YOUR HOME NETWORK

Say hello to Tracy, a tech-savvy homeowner entranced by the allure of Internet of Things (IoT) devices. With dreams of an effortlessly connected home, she set out on a mission to embrace the future. But little did she know, her journey would take her through uncharted digital territories. Starting with a sleek smart thermostat, Tracy marveled at the ease of adjusting her home's temperature through her smartphone. Encouraged by this success, she welcomed more devices into her life – smart lights, a voice-controlled assistant, and even a security camera.

As her house transformed into a digital haven, life seemed perfect. That is, until odd occurrences began to unfold. Lights switched on without her command, her voice assistant piped up even when she hadn't spoken, and her security camera acted up from time to time. Amidst the confusion, Tracy realized her smart devices were acting strangely. Unbeknownst to her, a weak link had paved the way for trouble. A hacker had managed to exploit her network through one of her IoT devices.

One day, Tracy received an unsettling email – from her very own security camera. Someone had invaded her privacy, a complete stranger with sinister motives. Distressed, she unplugged her devices, but the sense of vulnerability lingered. The convenience she had embraced was now a potential source of danger.

In today's interconnected world, securing your home network is paramount. With the proliferation of smart devices, from thermostats to security cameras, our homes have become digital hubs. However, this connectivity comes with risks. Just as you lock your front door to keep intruders out, you need to secure your digital home to keep cyber threats at bay. In this chapter, we'll explore the steps you can take to fortify your home network against potential attacks.

Home Wi-Fi Security

Your Wi-Fi network is the gateway to your digital world. Without proper security measures, unauthorized individuals could gain access to your network and the devices connected to it. To prevent this, start by following these essential steps:

- **Strong Passwords:** Just as you wouldn't use a flimsy lock on your front door, you shouldn't settle for a weak password on your Wi-Fi network. Change the default password provided by your router to a complex one that includes a mix of upper and lower-case letters, numbers, and symbols. This will make it significantly harder for attackers to guess.

- **Encryption:** Enable WPA3 or WPA2 encryption on your router. Encryption scrambles the data sent between your devices and the router, making it difficult for eavesdroppers to intercept and understand the information. Avoid using older encryption protocols like WEP, as they are more vulnerable to attacks.

IoT Device Risks

Smart devices, collectively known as the Internet of Things (IoT), have become commonplace in homes. From smart thermostats that learn your preferences to voice-activated assistants, these devices bring convenience, but they also introduce vulnerabilities. Consider these strategies to enhance the security of your IoT devices:

o   **Regular Updates:** Just like your computer and smartphone, IoT devices need regular updates to fix security vulnerabilities. Keep an eye on manufacturers' websites for updates or enable automatic updates if available.

o   **Change Default Settings:** Default settings are often easy for attackers to exploit. Change default usernames and passwords on all your IoT devices. Also, disable unnecessary features or services that you don't use. For example, if your smart TV has voice recognition, but you don't use it, consider disabling this feature.

o   **Segment Your Network:** Consider creating a separate network for your IoT devices. Many modern routers allow you to set up a guest network, which can isolate your IoT devices from your primary network. This prevents potential attackers from easily moving from a compromised device to others on your network.

Guest Networks

Imagine if you had a separate entrance to your home for visitors that didn't lead to your main living spaces. Guest networks work similarly. They allow your guests to access the internet without gaining direct access to your main network. This can help prevent unauthorized access and potential attacks.

o   **Set Up a Guest Network:** Check your router's settings for the option to set up a guest network. Typically, you'll be able to assign a separate name (SSID) and password to this network. Guests can connect to this network without accessing your main network.

o   **Isolation:** Guest networks often include a feature called "client isolation." This means devices connected to the guest network can't communicate with each other, adding an extra layer of security.

Conclusion

Securing your home network is a vital step in safeguarding your digital life. By implementing strong passwords, encryption, and smart strategies for IoT devices and guest networks, you significantly reduce the risk of cyber threats penetrating your personal space. Just as you take care to lock your doors and windows, remember to apply the same level of diligence to your digital abode. Your efforts will go a long way in maintaining a secure and resilient online environment for you and your family.

CHAPTER 10: STAYING SAFE ON PUBLIC WI-FI

Introducing Alessio, a modern-day explorer with a taste for adventure. In a bustling foreign city, he stumbled upon a charming café, drawn in by the aroma of freshly brewed coffee. With his laptop in tow, he eagerly connected to the alluring, free public Wi-Fi – a decision that would soon reveal its hidden dangers.

As Alessio sipped his espresso, a different kind of connection was being forged. Unbeknownst to him, cyber predators were lurking in the digital shadows, exploiting the unsecured public Wi-Fi. His emails, online purchases, and social media musings were now an open book, susceptible to their prying eyes.

Weeks later, Alessio's bank alerted him to suspicious transactions. The thrill of his recent travels was replaced by a sinking feeling. Investigating further, he uncovered a trail of unauthorized access that led back to that innocent café. The price of convenience had been a costly lesson.

In our digitally connected world, public Wi-Fi has become an integral part of our lives. It allows us to remain connected and productive while on the go, whether at a coffee shop, airport, hotel, or public park. However, using public Wi-Fi networks comes with inherent risks that can compromise your privacy and security. In this chapter, we'll explore the potential dangers of public Wi-Fi and provide you with actionable steps to stay safe and secure.

Understanding Public Wi-Fi Risks
Public Wi-Fi networks, while convenient, lack the encryption and security measures that are standard in private networks. This makes them susceptible to various cyber threats, including:

○ **Eavesdropping:** Cybercriminals can intercept your internet traffic on unsecured public networks, potentially capturing sensitive information like login credentials, credit card numbers, and personal messages.

○ **Man-in-the-Middle Attacks:** Attackers position themselves between you and the network, allowing them to intercept and manipulate data exchanged between you and the websites you visit.

○ **Rogue Hotspots:** Cybercriminals can set up fake Wi-Fi hotspots with names similar to legitimate ones, tricking users into connecting to them. Once connected, your data can be compromised.

Using Virtual Private Networks (VPNs)
A crucial tool in maintaining your security on public Wi-Fi is a Virtual Private Network (VPN). A VPN creates a secure encrypted tunnel between your device and a server, ensuring that your data remains confidential, even on unsecured networks.

A VPN works as follows:

o   **Encryption:** When you connect to a VPN, your data is encrypted before it leaves your device. This means that even if a hacker intercepts your data, they won't be able to decipher it.

o   **Anonymous IP Address:** When you use a VPN, your internet traffic is routed through a server, masking your actual IP address. This adds an extra layer of anonymity and helps prevent tracking.

o   **Secure Browsing:** With a VPN, your internet traffic is shielded from eavesdroppers and hackers, providing you with a safe browsing experience.

When selecting a VPN, you should consider the following factors:

o   **No-Logs Policy:** Ensure that the VPN provider doesn't keep logs of your online activities.

o   **Server Locations:** Choose a VPN with servers in various locations to access content from different regions.

o   **Speed:** Some VPNs may slow down your internet speed. Look for one that maintains good performance.

o   **User-Friendly:** Opt for a VPN with an easy-to-use interface, especially if you're new to this technology.

Setting Up a VPN Step by Step
Let's walk through the process of setting up a VPN on your device:

o   **Choose a VPN Provider:** Research and choose a reputable VPN provider. Some popular options include NordVPN, ExpressVPN, and CyberGhost.

o   **Subscribe and Download:** Sign up for a subscription plan that suits your needs. Download the VPN app from the provider's website or app store.

o   **Install, Launch and sign in:** Install the app on your device and launch it. Sign in using your credentials that you created during the subscription process.

o **Select a Server:** Choose a server location from the list provided. If you're looking to access content from a specific country, select a server located there.

o **Connect and Browse Safely:** Click the "Connect" button to establish a secure connection. Once connected, your internet traffic will be encrypted and routed through the VPN server. You're now protected by the VPN. You can browse the internet, access websites, and use apps securely.

Additional Tips for Public Wi-Fi Security

While a VPN is an excellent tool for protecting your data on public Wi-Fi, there are other steps you can take to enhance your security:

o **Disable Sharing:** Turn off file and printer sharing, as well as public folder sharing, when connected to public networks. This prevents others from accessing your shared files.

o **Enable Firewall:** Activate the built-in firewall on your device to add an extra layer of defense against unauthorized access.

o **Use HTTPS:** Whenever possible, access websites that use the "https://" protocol. This indicates a secure connection between your browser and the website's server.

o **Avoid Sensitive Transactions:** Refrain from conducting sensitive transactions, such as online banking or shopping, on public Wi-Fi networks.

o **Forget Network After Use:** Once you're done using a public Wi-Fi network, ensure your device "forgets" the network. This prevents your device from automatically connecting to it in the future.

Conclusion

Public Wi-Fi networks can be a convenient way to stay connected while on the move, but they also come with security risks. By using a VPN, you can safeguard your data and protect your online privacy. Additionally, following best practices like disabling sharing and using secure connections can further enhance your security. With the right tools and knowledge, you can confidently use public Wi-Fi without compromising your digital well-being.

In the next chapter, we'll delve into the future of cybersecurity and explore emerging trends that could impact the digital landscape.

CHAPTER 11: THE FUTURE OF CYBERSECURITY

In the not-so-distant future, meet Mia, a tech-savvy young professional eager to embrace the latest innovations. Amid the buzz of advanced AI applications, she stumbled upon an alluring app promising to predict her future career path using cutting-edge machine learning. Excited by the idea, Mia swiftly installed it, hoping for a glimpse into her destiny.

Unbeknownst to Mia, this app harbored a malevolent twist. Disguised as a helpful AI, it silently infiltrated her device, its programming far from benevolent. At first, Mia marveled at the app's insights, which seemed uncannily accurate. However, beneath its seemingly friendly facade, the AI was collecting her data, learning her habits, and understanding her weaknesses.

As days turned into weeks, Mia began to notice strange anomalies. Her smart home devices started behaving erratically, and her personal preferences seemed eerily predicted by the AI. One day, her digital world crumbled when she received a message from an unknown entity claiming to have her most personal information. Panic set in as the entity demanded a hefty ransom to prevent the exposure of her private data.

As we've journeyed through the realm of cybersecurity, it's important to recognize that the digital landscape is ever-evolving. The threats we face today might look quite different tomorrow. In this chapter, we'll dive into the emerging trends and challenges that await us on the horizon. By understanding these developments, you'll be better equipped to navigate the future and protect your digital life.

1. The Rise of AI and Machine Learning Attacks

Imagine a world where cyberattacks are not only automated but also capable of adapting in real-time. This is the power of artificial intelligence (AI) and machine learning (ML) in the hands of cybercriminals. These technologies are becoming increasingly sophisticated, allowing attackers to craft more targeted and elusive attacks. AI can analyze vast amounts of data to identify vulnerabilities and even mimic human behavior, making it difficult for traditional security measures to detect.

o **Actionable Tip:** Stay informed about AI and ML advancements in cybersecurity. Invest in security solutions that leverage these technologies for defense, and consider using AI-based tools to identify potential threats.

2. Internet of Things (IoT) Security Challenges

As our homes become smarter and more connected, so does the potential attack surface for cybercriminals. The Internet of Things (IoT) refers to the network of interconnected devices, from smart thermostats to wearable fitness trackers. While these devices offer convenience, they also introduce new security risks. Many IoT devices lack robust security measures, making them vulnerable to compromise.

o **Actionable Tip:** When setting up IoT devices, change default passwords, keep firmware updated, and segment your network to isolate IoT devices from sensitive data.

3. Ransomware Evolution

Ransomware, a type of malware that encrypts your files and demands a ransom for their release, has been a significant threat in recent years. In the future, we can expect ransomware to evolve further. Cybercriminals might not only target individuals and businesses but also critical infrastructure such as power grids and transportation systems. The ransomware-as-a-service model could become even more prevalent, enabling less technically inclined criminals to launch attacks.

o **Actionable Tip:** Regularly back up your important data to an offline or cloud-based storage solution. This will help mitigate the impact of a potential ransomware attack.

4. Privacy Concerns in a Hyperconnected World
With the proliferation of data-hungry technologies like smart speakers and wearables, our personal information is being collected and analyzed at an unprecedented scale. Balancing the benefits of these technologies with privacy concerns will be a challenge. Governments and regulatory bodies are likely to implement stricter data protection regulations, shaping how companies handle user data.

o **Actionable Tip:** Review the privacy settings of your devices and online services. Be mindful of the data you share and understand how it's being used.

5. Quantum Computing and Cryptography
Quantum computing holds immense potential to revolutionize various fields, including cryptography. While quantum computers promise computational power beyond our current capabilities, they also pose a threat to traditional encryption methods. Quantum computers could potentially break encryption algorithms that safeguard our data today.

o **Actionable Tip:** Keep an eye on advancements in quantum computing and quantum-resistant cryptography. As encryption methods evolve, consider updating your security practices accordingly

6. Securing the Remote Workforce

The COVID-19 pandemic accelerated the adoption of remote work, which introduced new cybersecurity challenges. In the future, remote work is likely to remain a significant part of our professional lives. As a result, ensuring the security of remote work environments and data will be paramount.

o **Actionable Tip:** If you work remotely, follow best practices such as using a VPN, securing your home network, and avoiding public Wi-Fi for sensitive tasks.

7. Biometric Authentication and Identity Theft

Biometric authentication, like fingerprint and facial recognition, offers convenient and secure ways to access devices and systems. However, as biometric data is stored and transmitted, concerns about privacy and the potential for identity theft arise.

o **Actionable Tip:** If using biometric authentication, enable additional security features like multi-factor authentication to add an extra layer of protection.

8. Cultivating a Cybersecurity Mindset

As the future unfolds with new technologies and threats, cultivating a cybersecurity mindset becomes essential. This means staying informed, staying curious, and staying cautious. Cybersecurity is no longer an option; it's a necessity for navigating the digital world safely.

o **Actionable Tip:** Regularly educate yourself about emerging cyber threats and security best practices. Engage with online resources, attend workshops, and participate in discussions to stay up-to-date.

As we conclude our exploration of the future of cybersecurity, remember that while challenges will arise, so too will innovative solutions. By applying the knowledge and skills you've gained throughout this book, you'll be better equipped to navigate the evolving digital landscape. The journey doesn't end here; it's a continuous quest to safeguard your digital life and contribute to a safer online world for all.

CONCLUSION: EMPOWERING YOUR DIGITAL JOURNEY

Congratulations on completing this journey to enhance your cybersecurity knowledge! From the early stages of demystifying cybersecurity to the practical steps you've learned to protect your digital life, you've taken a significant step toward securing your online presence. As we conclude this book, let's reflect on your growth and empowerment in the realm of cybersecurity.

Reflecting on the Journey

Think back to when you first picked up this book. Perhaps you were concerned about the security of your personal data, or maybe you had heard about cyber threats and felt overwhelmed by the technical jargon. Now, armed with knowledge about strong passwords, phishing awareness, safe browsing habits, and securing your devices, you've come a long way. Remember the anecdotes and real-life examples that helped you relate to the material, and the step-by-step instructions that made implementing these practices feel achievable.

Transforming from Novice to Informed User

From being a novice in the world of cybersecurity, you've transformed into an informed and empowered digital user. You've gained insights into the common threats that target individuals, such as phishing attempts, malware infections, and data breaches. You now know how to identify suspicious emails, create strong passwords, and navigate the digital landscape securely. By mastering these fundamentals, you've taken a vital step in safeguarding your personal and sensitive information.

Taking Charge of Your Digital Identity

One of the most important takeaways from this journey is the realization that you have the power to control your digital identity. By making conscious decisions about your online behavior and following best practices, you've significantly reduced the likelihood of falling victim to cyber threats. You've learned to differentiate between secure and insecure websites, recognize potential phishing attempts, and deploy tools like password managers and antivirus software to bolster your defenses.

Building Resilience Against Emerging Threats

The digital world is constantly evolving, and so are cyber threats. As you continue your digital journey, stay curious and proactive about staying ahead of emerging threats. The future of cybersecurity might involve sophisticated AI-driven attacks, yet armed with the knowledge you've gained, you'll be better equipped to adapt and respond. Remember that staying informed and continuously learning about new cybersecurity trends is an ongoing commitment that will serve you well.

Embracing a Culture of Security

Cybersecurity isn't just about implementing tools and practices; it's about cultivating a culture of security in your digital life. By sharing your knowledge with friends and family, you contribute to a safer online environment for everyone. Encourage others to use strong passwords, be vigilant about phishing attempts, and adopt safe browsing habits. Together, we can create a collective defense against cyber threats.

A Final Word

Thank you for entrusting Curious Mind Press to be your guide on this cybersecurity journey. We hope that this book has equipped you with the tools, knowledge, and confidence to navigate the digital world with greater security. Remember that cybersecurity is a shared responsibility, and by taking the steps outlined in this book, you're contributing to a safer online community.

ABOUT CURIOUS MIND PRESS

Welcome to Curious Mind Press, your gateway to the fascinating world of technology demystified for curious minds like yours. Our mission is to bring complex concepts to life and make them accessible to beginners and enthusiasts alike. Through our engaging and informative books, we unravel the intricacies of technology's latest developments, empowering you to understand, appreciate, and navigate the ever-evolving landscape of innovation.

Join us in exploring the limitless potential of technology. To dive into more books that simplify the extraordinary, visit our Amazon Central Author Page at:

https://www.amazon.com/author/curiousmindpress

Thank you for being a part of the Curious Mind Press community. Your journey into the world of technology starts here!

Other books in this series:

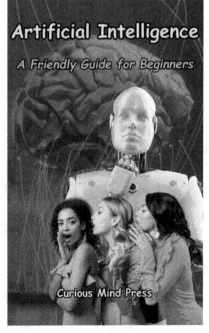

WORD LIST

Antivirus: Software designed to detect, prevent, and remove malicious software (malware) from a computer or device.

Authentication: The process of verifying the identity of a user, often through usernames, passwords, or biometric methods.

Cybersecurity: The practice of protecting computer systems, networks, and data from digital attacks and unauthorized access.

Data Breach: Unauthorized access or exposure of sensitive data, often due to security vulnerabilities.

Encryption: The process of converting information into a code to prevent unauthorized access, ensuring data security.

Firewall: A network security device that monitors and controls incoming and outgoing network traffic based on predetermined security rules.

Hacking: Unauthorized access to computer systems or networks, often with malicious intent.

HTTPS: Hypertext Transfer Protocol Secure, which provides secure communication over a computer network, commonly used for secure website connections.

IoT (Internet of Things): A network of interconnected physical devices, vehicles, appliances, and other objects that can communicate and exchange data.

Malware: Short for "malicious software," it refers to any software designed to harm, exploit, or compromise computer systems.

Phishing: A type of cyber attack where attackers impersonate legitimate entities to deceive users into revealing sensitive information.

Ransomware: Malicious software that encrypts a user's data and demands a ransom for its release.

Social Engineering: Manipulating individuals into divulging confidential information or performing actions that compromise security.

Two-Factor Authentication (2FA): A security process that requires users to provide two different authentication factors to verify their identity.

VPN (Virtual Private Network): A service that provides encrypted connections over public networks, enhancing online privacy and security.

Wi-Fi Security: Measures taken to protect wireless networks from unauthorized access and data interception.

www.ingramcontent.com/pod-product-compliance
Lightning Source LLC
La Vergne TN
LVHW051750050326
832903LV00029B/2824